WE GIVE SUPPORT, NOT ADVICE

WE GIVE SUPPORT, NOT ADVICE

MATTY BENNETT

QUEERMOJO
A Rebel Satori Imprint

New Orleans

Published in the United States of America by
Rebel Satori Press
www.rebelsatoripress.com

Paperback ISBN: 978-1-60864-211-3
ebook ISBN: 978-1-60864-223-6
Library of Congress Control Number: 2022945002

I love skipping anything casual—"hi, how are you, it's been forever"—and getting straight to the center of pain. Or happiness.

—Alex Dimitrov

[Affinity Group Guidelines]

The purpose of the **[Jefferson High School] [LGBTQ affinity group]** is to let members of the community know they are not alone. This will be achieved through open and honest communication where members can share their experiences, connect with one another, and build community. **[Insert current pronoun guidelines here.]**

Meetings will take place in **[Room 404, the old choir room across from the bathrooms]** on **[Mondays after school]**.

The faculty advisor(s) for **[current school year]** will be **[X]**.

The following guidelines and resources, created by the Fairview Public School District Administration Liaisons for Diversity, Equity, & Inclusion, should be used to effectively run the affinity space, acknowledging that individual groups will interpret and use the guidelines in their own ways:

[Affinity Group Guidelines]

The purpose of the **[Jefferson High School] [LGBTQ affinity group]** is to let members of the community know they are not alone. This will be achieved through open and honest communication where members can share their experiences, connect with one another, and build community. **[Insert current pronoun guidelines here.]**

Meetings will take place in **[Room 404, the old choir room across from the bathrooms]** on **[Mondays after school]**.

The faculty advisor(s) for **[current school year]** will be **[X]**.

The following guidelines and resources, created by the Fairview Public School District Administration Liaisons for Diversity, Equity, & Inclusion, should be used to effectively run the affinity space, acknowledging that individual groups will interpret and use the guidelines in their own ways:

[LGBTQ Affinity Group Sign-Up Sheet]

Preferred Name	Grade	Pronouns
Denice	12	she/they
Johnny	11	he/him
Finn	10	they/them, he/him
Angel	11	tf?
Lexie	9	she/her
Vivian	11	she/her

[Part 1]

[First, begin with the group guidelines.]

We enter slowly, creeping
into the old choir room
like it's a haunted house.
We curve our necks around the door frame,
silently exchanging nods
and faint smiles with one another.

We stand in the vastness
of the room, the wide,
dusty windows, the old piano
covered with a sheet.
We are immobile, a game
of freeze tag we've all lost.

Denice begins to unroll
a white poster with black letters.
We press our hands
against the cracked wall,
smooth the crumpled guidelines,
confirm our space.

We are not producers,
we are consumers of content
someone else came up with—
an administrator, probably.

We are readers, we are
semi-strangers, we are

huddled around this
neatly made poster to focus:
on the challenges
and feelings associated
with coming out as
gay, lesbian, bisexual, or transgender.

There's a spotted hawk
outside the window.
"Bitch is huge," Angel says.
We're all staring, wide-eyed,
darting back and forth between
the animal outside and the posted guidance,

line after line of letters forming
abstractions we can't yet make concrete
with our stories. The hawk hops a bit,
adjusts itself on the branch
outside our fourth-floor window
before gliding into the air.

The hawk circles our school,
and we're unsure if it's protecting
or hunting. The wrinkled list of guidelines
reminds us it can be used

to respond to distractions—
are we ready to begin?

[Then, ensure understanding of roles.]

There are no adults in the room.
We're pretty sure
there should be adults in the room.
"Where the teachers?"
We shrug.
Denice, Johnny, Finn, Angel, Vivian.
We're all waiting, in silence.
A sloppy circle, navy blue plastic chairs,
choir stands—this was the music room
before they cut music.
There's dust and cobwebs,
as if someone decorated for Halloween.
We're the ones who don't play a team sport
in the fall, or ever,
and there's no school play happening—
there might be one in the spring, they say.
We have time before we need
to do our homework,
or go to our part-time job,
or smoke weed in the thick trees
of the park behind the school.
When we say *we*, we mean the six of us,
now that Lexie has entered.
This is our spare hour
to glance at each other's eyes

in a makeshift geometric shape
that should resemble a circle,
though it appears as a hexagon.
The September light
through the dusty windows
is warm, rests on our hands folded
in our laps, gives us something to think about
while no one says or does anything.

[If numbers are low, make sure the school knows
your group exists.]

On the agenda today
at the school assembly is—sex.
Specifically, the difference between

gender and sex. Yes, in this auditorium
we're still talking about gender vs. sex,
not because we don't know the difference,

but because this is the hot-button issue
of our lifetime. Some folks can't seem
to get through a conversation

without saying cowboy or cowgirl.
So now they must say
cow*people*? The absurdity!

We hear—"Settle down,
ladies and gentlemen." "I always get
tongue-tied on the alphabet soup!"

"We have a gender-neutral bathroom
now." "Remember those pronouns.
I know it can be hard."

"Thanks for listening.
Who's ready for the football game
Friday evening!?"

This crowd is—exploding in cheers.
We're part of the crowd
and not, disappearing

and sticking out like a cowlick.
At the conclusion, auditorium doors
thrust open, straight lines of students

blurring into blobs, returning to a world
full of promise, a world full of
"you're so gay, bro" as we emerge,

but we feel a brush against
our shoulders. We see each other. We're
here—there's a little spark of joy.

Denice is—our leader,
unofficially. She's our
basketball player, general badass,

only senior. Her brother Danny
died her sophomore year, was killed
in gang-related gun violence

outside our school. Danny wasn't in a gang,
he was a bird perched
on a street sign. Walker Avenue.

We didn't know it was him until later.
We wondered, as we filed out
of the building after our two-hour lockdown,

who's responsible for
cleaning up the blood? Denice
started weightlifting. She's our

protector. She uses she/her or they/them,
and she'll beat the shit out of you
if there's a good reason.

8

She's the only one of us who understands
how birds vanish, how circles
are infinite, how to continue

despite being so tired.

[Get to know the physical space(s) the group will utilize.]

The old choir room—

We are gay, we are femme, we are loved
by our close friends and still
reeling from kindergarten bullying.

The gymnasium—

In P.E. class, some of us play like girls,
some of us play like boys, and either way
we aren't invited to play.

The school bathrooms—

We are always gendered, the gender-
inclusive bathroom is always locked, and we
don't like Mr. Martin, who has the key.

At home—

We are not femme, we are not masc., we wanted
that Tonka truck and that Barbie for our birthdays,
and we cried because they weren't for us.

In the hallways—

Between classes, we are stared at,
pointed at, laughed at, and sometimes it's hard
to find the strength to live.

The auditorium—

We're constantly dodging insults from
everyone because there's nothing about us
too insignificant to mock.

The parking lot—

We witness Denice's fist
form a comic book punch,
and we support her, from the window.

[As members become more vocal, remember to share airtime.]

Johnny is—an actor
wants to be the group leader
keeps bringing up the summer nights
we thought would never end that now feel far away
were a lifetime ago
although they were just last month
and Johnny wishes we could continue to live there
in those firefly nights
in grassy barefoot freedom
but the school routine feels marginally decent
like coming back to your pillow
after a long trip away from home.

Johnny says—it's too hot for school
the leaves should be changing
still they're firmly green
and we should be sipping hot coffee
but it's still iced
and those summer nights we'll long for all year
are replaced by circular conversations
about who we are and how we don't fit in
feeling in the moment we aren't growing
aren't learning
aren't doing much of anything.

Johnny says—we can't see the future
still we know the year will end eventually
and we'll be different somehow
based on whatever tragedy is the moment
based on whether or not we'll meet someone
who ignites our lungs like a gasoline-doused bonfire
based on our course load
based on the drama club's attic dance parties
based on the fact that time seems
to simultaneously drag us
and hurl us toward an amorphous abyss.

[Acknowledge the reason(s) the group exists.]

There's lots of silence

in our group—
silence we don't want,

silence we try to force

out, silence that
brings back memories

we wish we could forget,

but today,
Denice tells us to be

silent, for Adam.

Adam.
That was his name.

He was lanky, almost always

quiet in our classes.
Only a few of us knew him.

We remember him drinking
Mello Yello at lunch.

No one had any idea
the pain he was going through.

We're crying. No,

that's Lexie. Our heads
are down. No,

that's Finn & Vivian.

We're locking
sad eyes. No,

that's Johnny & Angel.

Denice says,
thank you for joining

in this moment
of silence. Let's begin.

Do we have anything to share?

Our hearts beat in our ears,
getting louder, closer, like a siren.

[Encourage participation, even when people are
hesitant to speak.]

Finn is—They/them. He/him.
New to school this year.
They came from a stretch
of desolate highway
through the slumping Appalachians.
They have no fond memories
from their old trailer park.

"Pass."

Finn is—knowledgeable, we think.
Finn says the term "transgender"
became popularized in the 1960s,
and anti-trans sentiments were used
to not hire trans people:
If you're looking for equal employment rights,
look employable!

"Pass."

Finn dreads—this place.
We see it on their face. Finn dreads
every place, it seems.
The gendered bathrooms, especially.

Black-painted nails, matte.
We talk about dread a lot.
We can't figure out how to make it go away.

"Pass."

Finn destroyed—the school's attempt
at fall decorations.
A sunflower tall as Finn,
round and big as their head, gripped
its thick stem and cracked it in half,
tossed it on the front steps of the school.
One of the front office ladies screamed.

"Pass."

Finn has—only answered
one ice-breaker question so far this year:
they want to be able to afford
the medical care they need,
and they want a humongous
late-night pizza.
Maybe someone to share a slice with.

[If there is no faculty advisor, find an English or
Humanities teacher.]

Ms. Chase is—here now. We're
polite, say hello, and she laughs, says
"You're welcome for saving the group!"

We don't laugh. She wants us to crack
open our ribs, use them
as a decorative bowl

in which she'll collect all of our
thoughts, written on parchment.
We are supposed to explain how

we got here. She says this will take
time. We feel rushed. She is trying
to prove she's one of the cool teachers,

thinks she's inherently good
for taking us on, thinks the sunlight
streaming across her

shoulder-length brown hair, the way
she sashays into the classroom
and flashes her white teeth,

the way she stretches her arm out the window
to catch a dying leaf before it falls to the earth
is all something true. A handsome view, sure,

but we will show her something real.
Something so fabulous and horrifying
she'll never be the same.

[Admin Activity #1:
Make a list of group intentions (bullets are fine).]

1. to find out who in the school is queer
   a. we're not trying to out people we just wanna know

2. to talk about sex
   a. lots of hoots & hollers
   b. a few groans

3. to listen to Lil' Nas X
   a. no objections

4. to debate who qualifies as a gay icon
   a. Cher yes
   b. #FREEBRITNEY
   c. Gloria Gaynor
      i. someone said who
         1. Denice is about to throw down
   d. Harry Styles
      i. now Denice is really about to throw down
         1. let's move on

5. to really talk about sex
   a. how does gay sex work, like, we have an idea but health class really did us dirty and did NOT give

us the tea!
- i. is it possible for Johnny to stop bringing this up every meeting?

6. to talk about the definition of sex
   - a. can you help us understand if we're virgins

7. to not talk about sex
   - a. we are so much more than sex
     - i. Vivian's ace arom

8. to talk about different identities
   - a. what is ace arom?

9. to educate straight people
   - a. is that even our job tho
     - i. no
     - ii. yes?
     - iii. no
     - iv. parking lot

10. to discuss our celebrity crushes

11. to make school more bearable
    - a. why is everyone so fucking mean?

12. to be here for one another

[Stay on task and be an active listener, even if it's difficult to do so.]

Angel is—a riot, in and out of class, big
curly hair, big attitude. In class, he yelled
at Sandra Cisneros for killing off a character
named Angel. "How fucking obvious is that?
Do better, Sandra." He got a day of
in-school suspension for that.

Angel seems—confused about
pronouns, but unlike the teachers, he says
"Shit, my bad," and moves on. No
restorative circle needed. Angel's always
got his phone plugged in. Sometimes
his mom doesn't pay the electric.

Angel is—gorgeous, a gleaming smile
that makes everyone a little crazy.
We can't be mad at someone who smiles so
genuinely, even after doing questionable things,
like climbing on top of the cabinets
in science class to take a nap.

Angel can't—wait to leave town.
He's saving up for a motorcycle
("Donor-cycles," Ms. Chase says. "Wear a helmet!"),

and he's ready to be anywhere
but here. We don't want him to
leave though. We're enamored with his light

brown eyes, his oversized t-shirts, his fast talk,
his dirty talk—Wait, no, that's just—

[It may be helpful to create a loose meeting schedule.]

FADE IN
INT. ROOM 404
MONDAY AFTERNOON

WE
form a locked door

WE
must knock to enter

WE
look toward Denice whenever there's hesitation

WE
appear as a circle of chairs

WE
hate icebreakers and would rather suffer the silence

WE
consider trying not to drown

WE
interrupt extended silence with a game of Skip-It

WE
don't hold hands or pray

WE
form a legacy for future queer kids

MS. CHASE
Oh, hello!—I'm here, friends!

WE
follow the guidelines, sometimes

WE
love Ru Paul and Laverne Cox

WE
don't love James Charles or Nikita Dragun

WE
make we-statements we don't always agree with

WE
solve for x: know it's anxiety, depression, or stress

JOHNNY
not everything can be solved

WE
roll our eyes, the truth still hurts

WE
give support, not advice

WE
need to be reminded of that many times

WE
stack the chairs in a matter of seconds and

WE

FADE OUT.

[Do not pressure anyone to share more than they're
comfortable with.]

Vivian is—not having it.
Today, or any day.
She calls us
sex-crazed maniacs.

There's more to us,
yes, we agree.
How much more?
We're not sure.

Vivian likes—getting
straight to the point.
No minced words.
Economy of language.

Coffee in hand.
Scalding. Purple scarf.
Pokémon fanatic.
Zero fucks given.

Vivian is—brilliant,
speaks 3 languages,
mumbles under her breath
in Mandarin when she's

pissed, which is a lot,
and speaks Spanish
with Angel & Denice
to talk shit on Ms. Chase.

Vivian wants—for us
to understand.
She's different.
She's not interested

in anyone. No sex.
Rare romance.
Still, she's here.
She's one of us.

[What happens in the group stays in the group.]

The other kids march
linearly, while we

wander around
the school in little eddies:

out of classrooms,
bathrooms, the gravel lot

behind the school
while skipping gym. We're

spinning around trees
so as to feel like

something is happening.
We are a quest

with no discernible
treasure. The places

we come out of hold
secrets, gloom.

None of us

are holding

hands in public.
On Tuesdays

we twirl. We've been
restored, slightly—

we're still lost but
with more flare.

By Wednesday, our
unity is but distance,

desperation for
one another and that

we'd all disappear.

[Confidentiality is top priority.]

Lexie is—a bit of a mess.
We're all a bit of a mess, to be fair,
but we're not wearing the same
overalls every day like Lexie.

Should we ask her about that?
She usually wears the same
green and yellow Hawaiian shirt
underneath the overalls.

Lexie runs her hands
over her long, brown braid
each time she speaks. It's one
of the ways she stays calm.

Lexie is—not queer. She's not gay.
She's not bi, or pan, or ace.
She's here as an ally.
She's said it twenty times now.

"Methinks thou dost protest too much,"
Angel mutters. Johnny punches his shoulder,
but wow, we love when Angel speaks
Shakespearean, even when it's problematic.

Lexie's having trouble breathing,
can we excuse her? "It's just—

my anxiety—

I get—

panic attacks—

I hate them—I'm

so sorry—

I'm not gay—

I'm flattered!—really,

thank you."

[Don't be afraid to speak up; vulnerability is key.]

Sometimes we don't speak
our minds, sometimes we sit
and we think
why are we here?

We think

Denice is the shit, think

everyone here can be really
stupid sometimes, think
we're going to keep saying
"pass" until someone calls us out.

No,
that's just Finn. We think
we should be allowed to play
our Nintendo Switches.

No,
that's Vivian. She wants to get a
shiny Espeon.

We think,
Yass, queen, preach! We think,
oh geez, another long,
boring story that literally

has no end in sight, think
you know who's looking fine tonight?
Seth Mosakowski.

No,

that's Johnny, he's obsessed
with *Mean Girls*. We think,
wow, this group is giving
us life, we think, wow,
someone who actually knows
what they're talking about.

We think
we finally feel like we've found
a home, and, also, only 10 minutes
until a phone break, think
we're gonna check who's slid
into our DMs really quick, just a glance,
we swear.

No, that's just
Johnny, again. We think
snaps and existentialism, you know?
We learned that
in English class, but we're still confused.

We think, let's normalize pansexuality,
and oh lawd,
Ms. Chase's talking about

the 90s again, it was so great,

blah blah,
we get it,

F this.

We're so tired,
but we'll be hitting different next week

and it's 4:00

and we'll see y'all after break.

[Part 2]

[Each person here is critical for success (or failure).]

Post Thanksgiving break—we carry extra weight
from turkey and the nasty things our family said.

Everyone's got a story and everyone's talking
at once. Calling us a circle won't make us

one. We're a blob. If the outside world were to think
about us, they might think: freaks, fags, weirdos,

ready to flee. The break was only five days,
but suddenly this room, this place, is where we say:

here is everything that happened to us. This room
is where our arms extend from our hearts

and form a collective, "Go team!" Phones away, eyes
pierced, we are ready for something. Calling us

healing won't heal us. We want the circles
under our eyes to fade, like a lover's whisper

as we fall asleep together on FaceTime. Calling us
the aftermath of a student's suicide, beauty out of

tragedy, feels disingenuous. To the front office,

the administrators, we are a box to check off: an *i*

to dot, a *t* to cross. We are 404, the old choir room
across from the bathrooms. The dusty music

stands, cobwebs in the corners. We are Monday
afternoons, and we are awkward looks as we pass

each other elsewhere. Everyone stares. We are not
elsewhere. We've done this all wrong, haven't we?

We've formed the circle with the navy blue chairs,
and now, finally, we'll say—welcome back.

[If the group is in an icebreaker rut, brainstorm some new ones together.]

Think of all the gay things
we could do if we were trapped
inside a forcefield.

Imagine?

So many of us died
in the 80s and 90s.
Does that mean our legacy is

death?

Due to our death, what's
the movie or show or song or dance
that doesn't exist today that

should?

There's so much stuff
in here—let's redecorate and
make it glam. How can we

not?

If love is love,
then why is it completely
impossible for us to

define?

What's the point of being
created if we didn't
ask for it—none of

us?

[The faculty advisor has full authority to take over the conversation.]

Today's ice breaker question:
If you could have lunch with any famous person,
dead or alive, who would it be and why?

Ms. Chase says:
"Ellen DeGeneres."
Angel scoffs, smoothly turns it into a cough.

No one's saying anything.
In the silence, Ms. Chase decides
we should go.

***

When we go to lunch with Ellen,
the entire restaurant is white.
There are white tablecloths,

wide open windows, and white
French doors bordered
by big white drapery rippling

in an ocean breeze.
The white sunlight fills the room

and dazzles the glassware on the tables.

Everything about Ellen
is white. She's wearing a white suit
with a white bow tie,

and she has perfect white teeth—
they sparkle every time
she laughs.

We all sit together
at a big circular table
with white plates and thick white napkins.

We drink white grape juice
out of wine glasses and we can't
stop laughing. Ellen is so funny.

The waiters dressed in white
collared shirts and white pants
and white aprons deliver us our food.

When the crisp green salads
are brought out, we laugh.
When the salmon with a side

of fresh asparagus is brought out,
we laugh. The waiters

laugh with us, too.

Ellen tells one of her classic jokes:
Why do ghosts hate going to prom?
Because they have no "body" to dance with.

This makes us laugh
and makes dealing with
the ghosts at the table easier.

The chairs at the table are plush and white
and so comfortable we could sink into them forever
and never leave. Who would ever want to leave?

Ellen, we used to wonder how you do it.
And now we know.
It's painted over everything.

[Admin Activity #2: Wellness Wheels]

Denice is 84% intellectually well,
colored in blue marker, thank goodness
she's so sharp, here to support us
through our society's normative issues.

Finn is 2% physically well,
orange marker, no physical changes
yet, someday soon, maybe,
but until then—

Lexie is 90% emotionally well,
green marker, not 100%, since, you know,
we still have so much work to do,
as allies, so we must be a bit unsatisfied.

Angel is 100% spiritually well,
yellow marker, says he's a peaceful spirit,
but—closed fist to open palm,
he'll protect us if we need it.

Vivian is 62% socially well,
purple marker, wishes people would
understand she is not "chemically imbalanced,"
and there's nothing wrong with her.

Johnny is 17% environmentally well,
red marker—"It's gross!"—the trash
in the street, the hallways, the classrooms,
the ceiling breaking across our desks.

We're holding up our wheels for all
to see, our wellness quantified in pie
slices, colors, and since it's just us,
Denice tells us to rip everything up,

and then, on three—one, two, three!—
hundreds of paper pieces thrust
into the air, colorful confetti floating
down over our faces. A red fragment

lands on Vivian's forehead, Johnny swats
at them all frantically, Angel & Denice
dance in the rainfall, Finn's unamused,
and after it's all settled on the carpet—

damn, we have to clean this up.

[Don't be afraid to tackle tough subjects (e.g., teenage drug use).]

Today, spirits clamber
out of open mouths,
situate themselves on the floor
in the form of autumn trees.

The circle has holes.

Outside, the rest of the school
cheers at the pep rally.
The football team's
final game is coming.

We block them out
with depression
and panic attacks.

"Pass."

We do not stumble
through our pronouns
anymore.

There's a painting
of an old white man

in the corner of the room.

He's got his hand clasped
across Vivian's mouth.

"Pass."

They, them, theirs.

Why did we put out 7 chairs today?
Ms. Chase is not here.

We carry oppression in our purses,
with some quarters for
the soda machine outside.

"Pass."

The only word Finn says all meeting.

When the silence is thick
at 3:26 p.m., Adam appears
in the empty chair,
legs and eyes crossed.

He's holding a can
of Mello Yello. He takes a big,
refreshing swig.

We miss you, Adam,
even though we didn't
really know you. Is that weird?

You have such
long legs, and we're doing
alright, thank you.

He nods.
It's been real.

He floats upward
and dissipates in the blades
of the ceiling fan.

[Encourage round-robin participation for any group activities.]

Johnny has an idea to tell a group story
as a fun bonding activity to get to know each other
a little better.

We like Johnny's idea, so we go round and round,
line by line:

Vivian:
"Once upon a time there was a little girl named
Jasmine."

Denice:
"Jasmine really wanted a bike for her birthday."

Finn:
"Pass."

Angel:
"Pssht. So Jazzy Jazz was like, I'm gonna set myself up
with a lemonade stand and make some stacks,
but her dumbass dad forgot to get her the lemonade
mix like she asked."

Johnny:

"Wow, OK. Um, so, luckily Jasmine had a lemon tree in her backyard because she lives in California, so she went out back to pick some lemons."

Lexie:

"Unfortunately, she was too short to reach the lemons, so she ran back inside to grab a chair to stand on."

Vivian:

"When she went inside, she saw her dad, lying in a pool of his own blood."

Lexie:
"What?"

Angel:

"Oh hell yeah, here we go, baby!"

Vivian:

"And she saw her mom with a knife."

Angel:

"Woah woah woah, wait your turn!"

Denice:

"I'm not doing the knife thing. I'm gonna say Jasmine thinks her dad tripped and hurt himself, so she called

911."

Finn:
"Pass."

Angel:
"Yeah right, so the cops come in and they're like, the fuck? You a bad little girl, we know you killed your father, and they drag her out of there, and she's crying and stuff, but really it was the mom who did it, and she's out on the run, gonna let her daughter take the fall because she's a—"

Johnny:
"OK! So, they realize it was all a misunderstanding, and actually the dad was playing a funny trick on them, and he was lying in a bunch of ketchup! The end."

Angel:
"What?"

Vivian:
"I don't think that's what happened."

Denice:
"Fun icebreaker, Johnny."

Johnny:
"You can't blame this all on me."

Angel:
"That was dope! Let's do another."

[Affinity groups foster closeness and togetherness.]

It's starting to lightly snow

the first snowfall of the year

which we love

and we're all looking

out at the fluffy flakes

oohing and aahing

when we notice

Johnny looking at Angel

Angel looking at Johnny

Johnny glancing away quickly

Angel glancing toward the door

their eyes locking once more

Denice's raised eyebrow

arching like the gateway to the West

Johnny and Angel locking eyes again

and we're reminded why we exist

[Let participants know the group is a safe space.]

We've been
given a rainbow

to place on the door.
A *safe space* sticker

from the admin.
We want our skin

to be covered
in paint,

and the colors
will blur, seep

into the creases
of our palms,

and we'll make
a mural

downstairs
in the main hallway.

We'll press our palms

to our cheeks,

give spirit fingers
to the world.

This will be
ours. And glitter.

Maybe the admin
will give us glitter next.

It's been almost a year
since Adam died.

Some of us are
still sad and some of us

are new and didn't
know who he was.

We've been
given a rainbow

flag to hang
from the ceiling.

We wonder
how he

did it, but
no one asks.

We wish
we'd been given rainbow-

colored condoms,
dental dams,

lots of them, so we
could plunge

our hands
into a bowl of them,

make them spill
over. What does

an open chest
cavity feel like?

Dear Adam,
can you tell us

where your
gravestone is

so we can show you
everything

you've created?

[Two faculty advisors are preferable, as the role can
be demanding.]

Ms. Chase is—not here, again. She says
she has a faculty meeting. We haven't seen her
in three weeks.

Denice is—here, always,
questioning us and herself,
but mostly herself today. Questioning

what she's allowed to question in front of us.
What is she allowed to not know?
Denice speaks as dawn breaking through naked trees.

We are always in awe. Her chair is the only one
that rolls, an old teacher's desk chair.
We often speak about Denice

as if she's some unsolved mystery.
Waiting to be cracked. We keep saying thank you,
and she's tired of that shit.

Why do we keep thanking her? She is us.
She is this circle. She needs us
like we need her. Denice stands,

announces her newest trick: balancing
all of our problems on her head
like a thick, yellow-stained dictionary.

Can someone help us help her with this balancing act?

[Use discretion and good judgment when speaking
about sex.]

Today we're a ring of fire

eyes poised and ready to erupt

so let's start with a question

about desire and sex and yes let's share

our top five celebrity crushes

We'll go into details and won't stop

but before we go around

let's get on our knees

and pray that when we consume

these words they'll fuel us

and urge our circle into a spiral

of flames from lips that rarely speak

because today we're ready

to desire out loud

so if we're burning we have to wait

until at least the last five minutes

to put us out with death

[Acknowledge important dates within the community.]

December 12th—
The date of Adam's death.

We put on our
regular school clothes
because we don't think
about how one day
we'll have no more days.
Today, we're intrigued
by a half-eaten
white cake
with pink flowerets
that Ms. Chase brought in,
left over from
a student's birthday.

We're creeping
toward winter break.

We stuff our faces,
and Finn's got cake
smeared across
their left cheek.
We settle in

to a winter afternoon
crisp as the edges
of freshly cut roses.
Sometimes we are ready
to talk and debate,
and sometimes
we are simply digesting.

[Being an active listener means re-focusing when
your mind wanders.]

One day
before we stack the chairs
but after
we sit in silence
for seven whole minutes
we imagine
the old choir from the 90s
singing a Mariah Carey melody
"Fantasy"
"Always be my Baby"
and of course "All I Want
for Christmas is You"
she's the comeback queen
she's the elusive chanteuse
and we forgive the choir
for butchering her high notes
and we think about
the meme of Mariah
returning to the sea
after her duties
as Christmas Queen
have finished for the year
and we let her pull us
into the ocean

the freezing water
right over our heads

[Construct a shared definition of the group, for
communal understanding.]

Ms. Chase is—back again. We never know
when she'll show. She says that this is our boudoir, our
sulking place. Angel's eyebrow says: *Our?*
This is our abattoir, our slaughterhouse.

We are rumbling, a building bass emanating
from the floor. Pulse. We hold our hands
behind our backs. Sometimes a fairy
flutters around, cuffing them for fun.

We said it before and we'll say it again:
we're consumers, and we're ready to be consumed.
We spill our stories onto the carpet
and don't worry about the stains.

We hope someone will clean us,
eventually. For now, the splotches and sputters
are a million little moments
of death. We take a shower in the vibrant red.

We must remember that we can sparkle.
Our power stance is hand to hip, chin high.
Bullets. Screams. We will speak of this
forever. We only seem to matter when we die.

[Part 3]

[Admin (Take-Home) Activity #3: Journaling over break.]

Name: Denice	
Journal Entry:	Christmas isn't the same since you died, Danny. I wish you were here, so badly. I still have your blue sweatshirt. Sorry I stole it from you. Our Christmas tree's got blue lights this year & blue ribbons. It's pretty, but the blue lights are making X's across my eyes. Pop's cradled in the recliner with his whiskey. You know. I keep asking myself, who was I before that lockdown, before you died? I remember you dancing crazy in the living room. Mom's working at the diner right now. I love her so much, and she loves me, but Pop doesn't, I swear. He doesn't love anyone anymore. He's not even trying — & I get it. It just sucks.

Name: Vivian	
Journal Entry:	I love being home for break. Usually I just hang in my room and play Pokémon, specifically Pokémon X on my old 3DS because I love the fairy type, and Xerneas is like the official pride Pokémon — its rainbow antlers are absolutely fabulous. People think I just study all the time, which I mostly do… I put so much pressure on myself during the school year though, so I like to just be a kid again on breaks. Sometimes, when I think about the others in the group, like Denice and Finn, I realize how much privilege I have. My parents are insanely supportive of me — They waited so long to adopt me, so I feel like they were just grateful to finally have a child. They are just the most loving, accepting parents ever. They've always encouraged me to explore my identity, and they talk openly with me about sex and gender and stuff. Why can't all my friends' parents be like that? OK, gotta go, we're watching The Polar Express now :)

Name: Johnny	
Journal Entry:	I love that lavish popcorn you only eat at Christmas, in those tins decorated with winter scenes—I'd like to jump inside one of those, ride in a horse-drawn sleigh. Ugh, it makes me feel a little guilty because I know Mom's splurging a bit, even though she shouldn't be. Things have been pretty tight since the divorce. TBH, I think I was too gay for Dad, and I was too much for their marriage. I don't know that for a fact, but sometimes it feels like that. I'm glad Mom moved on, but I'm def not in love with our new neighborhood. It's so run-down. My new school is a joke. Some teachers are OK but most are trash. Some of the boys are cute at least lol. I think I'm ready to have my first BF. I'm terrified to utter the words "I like you" tho. They feel… inaccurate? I don't "like" Angel. His existence gives me strength to roll out of bed. I'm listening to "Halo" by Beyoncé, and even her words don't feel like enough… I think that's how you know it's real.

Name: Finn	
Journal Entry:	This activity is asinine; however, I have nothing better to do at home over break. It's nice to relax though. The best thing about moving to a new school and a new state is that I'm Finn. I've always been Finn. No one knows me as Julie. Julie is d-e-a-d. Well, Aunt Lyla knows about Julie, but she has never misgendered me or called me the wrong name or used the wrong pronouns. The fact that she took me in when my parents gave up on me says a lot. The swiftness in which it happened is still shocking to me. Me: I'm trans. Them: goodbye. In the same breath. For a few weeks, I thought I wanted my life to be over. I thought no one would accept me as I truly am. I thought, there's no point in living if I can't be the person I'm meant to be. I'll never let them know it, but this move, Aunt Lyla, this group… they saved my life.

Name: Lexie	
Journal Entry:	There's not a ton to do over break. Hanukkah already happened, and we don't really celebrate Christmas. Maybe that's why I chopped off all my hair in the bathroom yesterday? I was bored? I don't know why I did it. I was just staring in the mirror, and two minutes later the person staring back had cut all her hair. I'm dissociating now. I don't know who I am. That braid has been my signature since kindergarten! Literally, who am I now? Why did I do that? What's wrong with me? Ugh, I miss everyone. They're kind of my main friend group now! Even though I'm not like them, it's so nice to be around them. They're so free. They're so... themselves. I want to be like that. I'm NOT a lesbian, or bi, but I love supporting my queer friends. And obviously like, yeah, if Zendaya asked me out on a date I would say yes. I mean, she's gorgeous. Anyway, this new cut is kinda growing on me... I feel 10 pounds lighter!

Name: Angel	
Journal Entry:	Mamá Juana is still at work, and I'm at home with my 4 little brothers and sisters. They're so damn loud. Estrella is the cutest but also the most evil, I swear. Damn, Juana needs to get home ASAP. I'm tryna sneak out and ride my SSR 125 dirt bike. I FINALLY GOT IT! OK, so it's not a motorcycle, but damn, that shit's expensive! I love my dirt bike tho. Juana was so pissed when she saw it. I didn't work at Dunkin for 300 hours to not buy a bike tho. I know I was supposed to give her most of the money I made, but I wanted it so bad. After about a week she chilled out, and she told me I'll drive "las chicas locas" with that thing. How can I tell her who I am? FUCK. I can't. I just can't. But then wtf am I supposed to do about — I can't even write his name. HIS name. God. Wtf am I going to do?

[During extended breaks, make sure members have a way to connect.]

Messages in the Group Chat on New Year's Eve:

Denice:
Happy New Year, y'all!

Angel:
IM DRUNK BITCHES

Johnny:
Thanks, Denice! <3
Happy New Year, everyone!!

Angel:
DONT IGNORE ME

Lexie:
happy new year :)

Vivian:
HAPPY NEW YEAR!
Angel let's party lol

Angel:
YAAAAAAASSSS

dance party
vaminooosss

Johnny:
Angel, go to bed.

Angel:
Only if u join me

Denice:
Oh lawd

Vivian:
vomit

Angel:
JOKES JUST JOKES

Vivian:
doubtful

Finn:
I'm putting this chat on mute. Good night.

Angel:
NOOOO FINN
COME BACK

Denice:
I can't wait to see y'all again.

Johnny:
Same here

Vivian:
frfr same

Angel:
SEE U SOON BBS

[Part 4]

[Second Semester, reassess group goals and
outcomes thus far.]

We are—returned. We keep

saying we didn't do anything
over break, yet Finn's hair
is blue, Lexie traded her braid
for a pixie cut, same overalls, Denice broke
her toe and gets to use the elevator

for a while, Vivian's still on her way back
from visiting family, and we all know
Johnny and Angel are in something—
we're not saying anything
about it though.

We are—withdrawn. Silent,

the physical differences speak
for themselves. We're all wearing
our coats. The heater's broken.
We've been shaking all day. Johnny's eyes
say to Angel *we could use body warmth*,

and now Angel has to go to the bathroom,
Johnny following closely behind. It's too

late. We are already changing,
minute by minute, at warp speed,
while we sit here, together, silent, and still.

LGBTQ AFFINITY GROUP—

Calling all LGBTQ students and allies! It's a new semester, and with that comes new stresses, new schedules, and maybe you need a fresh start! Have you been bullied for not fitting in? Have you been looking for a community? Have you been looking for a friend who understands what you're going through? Well, we hope you'll come join Jefferson's first LGBTQ affinity group. We meet every Monday afternoon in room 404, the old choir room across from the bathrooms, and we talk about all sorts of things, like gender, sexuality, bullying, issues we're facing, etc. We'd love to have more members. Reach out to Denice if you have any questions! Ms. Chase is our faculty advisor. We hope to see you there!

Lots of thunder and lightning today.
Finn says they're being bullied in gym class,
and our new guest—Advice Guy™—says Finn
should get stronger than the bullies
so they back down.
It's not that hard, you know.
Do we want to know about carbo-loading
and the best kinds of proteins to eat
to gain muscle mass?
No? Well,
we're hearing about it now anyway.
Another thunderclap.
It's so loud.
Should we take cover?
Usually there's not thunder and lightning in January.
According to Advice Guy™,
thundersnow is essentially harmless.
He's going to study meteorology next year
when he goes to college.
Just kidding, it's only a hobby.
He's watched lots of YouTube videos.
He's studying business, obviously.
That's the best way to make money.
Does everyone know about cryptocurrency?
It's the future.

Angel's imagining clocking Advice Guy™
right in his cleft chin.
Johnny's eyes are wide,
and he's shaking his head.
Vivian brought two new friends, May & Kim,
and they're not even paying attention.
They're playing *Pokémon Legends: Arceus*
on their Switches.
The lights flicker, and Lexie screams.
She hates storms.
She's calling her dad to come pick her up early.
Advice Guy™ says she's overreacting
and that everything will pass.
Men are more likely to get struck by lightning
anyway—"Probably because we're so brave
and don't worry about it, haha!
Maybe we should!"
Denice nods, slowly.
"Yeah, maybe you should."

[Silence is OK but keep encouraging participation.]

At this week's meeting, we're back

to the original six

and no one speaks. Maybe

it's an off day. Everyone is internal,

ruminating, and the silence

is our adversary. We are

disquieted and in danger.

Our opponent severs our heads

from our bodies. We look like

tiki torches. The world is going

black and we are losing everything.

Our bodies are gone. Heads spinning, eyes

wide and begging for an open mouth.

Denice? Johnny? Lexie? A throat clears,

a lighthouse. Maybe if we flare

our nostrils in unison we will be

victorious. We could snare the silence,

but our snaps need work. Last chance:

let's capture the silence in a steel crate,

make it our own. We could let it out

every six hours, promise it a decent life.

Or we could lean our heads back,

open our mouths wide and wait

for a primal scream to emerge.

[Try to keep distractions to the group at a minimum.]

When Kory walks through the door, time stops.
For Denice at least. Kory is Denice's ex.
Angel & Vivian initiate fight mode.
They know Kory cheated on Denice
with a softball girl from our rival high school,
and now we're collectively holding our breath,
except Lexie & Finn,
who have no idea what's going on.

"Hey," Kory says.
"Hey," Denice replies.

"Wow, riveting," Angel mutters.

We need more chairs.
Vivian says May & Kim aren't coming—
they didn't have very much fun.
Advice Guy™ enters, and Angel groans
like a pull-chain lawn mower.

Through the wall, we hear hoots & hollers
while we're sitting in some unbearable silence,
again, and Denice goes to investigate.

It's the video game club.

They connected a PS5 to the projector,
and they're playing an NBA game.

We share our names, pronouns,
and something interesting from our weekend—
"Angel, he/him, and I apologized to a friend
I'd been meaning to for a long, long time."
He glares at Kory.

The rigamarole is formulaic,
more awkward than usual.

"Can we talk?" Kory whispers.
Denice shrugs reluctantly, then tells the group
to start on the next activity
before heading into the hall.

We take a look at the worksheet activity
for a moment,
then rush to the door, ears plastered
to hear what's happening. We can't hear
anything. Advice Guy™ grabs
a cafeteria cup from his backpack.
Finally, something useful.

"I want you back, Denice."

Angel mouths to us: *oh no she did not.*

Vivian sends up a prayer in Mandarin
to give her strength.

There's a long silence————
we're all shrugging our shoulders.

"Maybe the old Denice from last year,
who was a hot mess
and emotionally unstable, would have
said yes. But this Denice—
I have to do
what's best for me, Kory.
I have to say no."

We rush back to the circle,
and Vivian starts reading the instructions
aloud as Denice comes back in.
She returns to the circle
and takes a deep breath
as she sits down.

"Welcome back, babe," Vivian says.
"You ready?"

Denice smiles.
"You know it."

[Admin Activity #4: Flipping the Coin]

Directions: Can you change the way you think by changing the words you use? Can you… "flip the coin"?	
Negative (–)	Positive (+)
Obstacle	Challenge
Cry-baby	In touch with their emotions… not sorry bout it!!
Aggressive	"said lil' b---- you can't f--- with me, if you wanted to" GOSPEL from Cardi B & now she's a millionaire so
Busy-body	Concerned about the well-being of friends.
Coward	Knows their limits!!! We stan.

Pushy	That one supportive friend who's there to say: oh honey, just do it and get it over with all ready
Timid	Some people are shy. Nothing wrong with this?? we don't need to flip.
Boring	This one's impossible, don't be basic AF!!!! That's the worst.

[Reminder: there should always be an adult present during affinity group.]

We offer to stack the chairs
when the meeting ends.
We minus Denice,
they head to the gym, we minus Finn,
they're catching the end
of anime club, we minus Vivian,
she heads to the library,
we minus Advice Guy™, he left
halfway through, we minus Lexie,
she gets picked up by her dad,
and two seconds
after the 404 room door creeps
to a close, our lips are pressed
against each other
as if they're magnetized,
and our heads are
balls of light, no
oxygen, inhaling
each other to stay
alive, and Ms. Chase bursts
through the door and gasps:

"Oh my!"

All our eyes are wide
circles of white and brown
and Ms. Chase is still standing
in the doorframe
like a stock photo for shock,
and we're no longer
a *we*, we are Johnny
and Angel and Ms. Chase and
silence and a room
that should have been
empty and we are unsure
what happens now.

[Take a few minutes to summarize each meeting.]

We live on a spectrum of anger
and apathy. When we are fed

guilt, we bloat, but not
completely uncomfortable. We

become large and somewhat
immobile, a clunker. We

can still run though. When we get
left behind, in the gravel lot, our faces

get covered in dirt. This is not the case
for the other kids. We often eat dirt.

We say, it's sour or bitter or
iron-like. Please, don't leave us

in the dirt, we say. We say, where we start
is tolerance. Another word: bullshit.

Acceptance: also bullshit. It's time
to celebrate ourselves or nothing

at all. Every day we choose anger
because it's not useless: it fuels us.

[Restorative circles are necessary if rules are broken.]

Ms. Chase's fluorescent lights glare like we're
in the E.R., and we assume this conversation
will be as predictable as the posters she's got

on the walls of her social studies classroom:

W—hen you
E—nter this room
L—earning is fun &
C—ooperation is expected
O—ur positive attitude &
M—utual respect are part of
E—verything we do & say

Angel makes a gagging gesture while Ms. Chase
pulls out a sheet of paper to take notes.

She places her clasped hands gently on her desk.
Angel mirrors her exact motions and smiles.
We stare intensely at Ms. Chase, looking for a signal

that shows how she really feels about us.

Her yellow blouse has ruffles around the collar,
which undercuts her stern, furrowed brow.

Ms. Chase begins: "Yesterday, I sat in my sunroom,
enjoying a cup of coffee. It's how I start
every Sunday morning, naturally. From the window,

I saw a young father carrying his baby.
He suddenly slipped on some leftover ice
from the night's prior snow, and he fell

on top of the baby. I screamed! I gasped!
I was frozen, stunned. I was so concerned
for the little baby! But to my surprise,

when the young father stood up, the baby
wasn't even crying. Somehow, the baby
wasn't hurt in the slightest. The young father

went to the car, put the baby in the car seat,
and he drove off like nothing happened,
and I was left with the shock that I felt,

then the realization that everything was OK."
Our eyes are wide open, darting around
the classroom. After a long pause, in which Ms. Chase

When he opens them, the bus pulls away,
and the red taillights
blur into a flurry of snow.

is clearly waiting for our acknowledgement
that we understood the story, she says:
"This can't happen again. You understand that, right?"

A strand of white among Ms. Chase's brown hair
shimmers in the light. Angel and Johnny glance
at each other, then back to Ms. Chase again.

We're an equilateral triangle, strong, purposeful
in our positions—nodding. "Sure, we understand,"
Angel starts, "but let me ask you something,

Ms. Chase… If you had found a boy
and a *girl* kissing in the room, would you have
some bullshit restorative circle for them, too?"

Johnny's mouth falls open in shock and amazement,
and Angel looks smug. All the cheer and blood has
drained from Ms. Chase's face. Angel stands to leave.

"See ya at the next meeting?"

[Stay as a whole group as much as possible; avoid sub-groups.]

Underneath the streetlamp at the bus stop,
it's lightly snowing—
a calm, peaceful, navy blue night.

"I can't believe you told Ms. Chase off like that!
Oh my God!" Johnny paces back and forth
while Angel sits on the bus stop bench.

"She had it coming."
Angel flips up the collar of his puffy black coat.

Johnny takes a sharp inhale of cold air.
"Does this mean you—that we could—
go public? I don't want to hide."

There's a poster taped to the streetlamp
for a missing black cat named Desi.
Angel stands, moving out into the snow.
He leans his head back to catch snowflakes
on his tongue. Johnny gives him a light shove.

"I'm serious. I don't want to do this
if we have to hide from everyone."

Johnny turns to look over his shoulder
and sees the bus approaching.

"Are you ever going to tell your mom?"

Johnny and Angel hold each other's gaze
for a few moments, lingering,
waiting for magic words
to swirl around them like a snow globe,
waiting for an embrace of possibility—

waiting————

Angel breaks

and

looks down at the slushy, gray street.

The bus pulls up next to them,
lowers slightly as the door opens.

Angel shrugs his shoulders.

"I gotta go."

Johnny squeezes his eyes shut.

[Bring in outside voices to lead the group whenever possible.]

Mr. Vasquez is an administrator from the district, and he's here with us today. He's got a sharp dark blue suit, pink pocket square, golden glasses, and the sides of his head are almost shaved, with tight, curly black hair on top.

We're quite smitten—no, that's just Johnny. He's scooted his chair closer than normal. Ms. Chase is here too, on the other side. Angel's not here—again. Lexie, Vivian, Finn, and Denice are all politely present for our first-ever guest speaker.

Mr. Vasquez tells us to call him "Friend Antonio," and for today, he wants to impart some wisdom. He tells us this group that we have here is something special, something *spectacular*, something he didn't have when he was a teenager.

The way Friend Antonio says the word— *specTACular*—with such grandeur, makes us stop. We're all thinking about the word spectacular now. Johnny's thinking about pageantry, how he should start writing *LGBTQ Affinity Group: The Musical*.

Finn's thinking about the mountain views
back home, the only thing that gave them a sense
of hope, and if they'll ever see them again.
Lexie's thinking how we're so large, we keep
expanding, growing, people noticing——

Denice is thinking how we're a *spectacle*,
and, though he means well, Friend Antonio is
an outsider looking in on what it means to be
a queer teenager today. Vivian's thinking about
spectacles—she wants some new Warby Parkers.

Friend Antonio is gay and single, and we're
fascinated: *He's like 40, right? Shouldn't
40-year-olds be married? Seems old
to not be married.* Many of us think this
but don't say it out loud.

Friend Antonio tells us about coming of age
as a gay man in the late 90s. There was so much
shame and fear associated with AIDS then,
and that still affects him today. He wasn't out
as gay when he was a teenager.

He didn't come out until the mid-2000s
when things were really starting to get better.
Later in life, he came out as HIV-positive,
and in some ways, this was a more difficult

coming out—but he's happy, healthy, and thriving.

He says he saw a show called *Queer as Folk*
in the early 2000s; this helped him, and even though
the representation was overwhelming white,
it was still wonderful to see gay men living
their lives in somewhat mainstream media.

Johnny asks about *Love, Simon* and *Heartstopper*
and if Friend Antonio has read or seen either of these,
and he says yes, he has, and how great it is to have
such positive representations for queer youth today,
and, also, he's a little jealous *he* didn't have that.

Today, it fills him with such pride to see us living
as our authentic selves. Every beautiful,
progressive thing he witnesses for our queer youth
fills him with a melancholic happiness—how badly
he wishes he could do it all again today.

There are so many ways Friend Antonio is different
from us, generationally, and through his experiences,
and yet, after today, after our meeting, each one of us
hugs him—even Finn—before saying goodbye,
and Friend Antonio is a part of our *we*, indefinitely.

[If any members become chronically absent, check
in on them.]

Ode to the hot March day
none of us were expecting
it exploded
in all of us
wild dance party
outside the front of the school
after classes
for an afternoon
we danced and our we
expanded

Ode to the off-brand Dayquil
we're taking shots of
this week
now that we're back
to freezing temperatures
and thumbprint snowflakes

Ode to the fact
that both Angel & Johnny
have strategically skipped affinity group
on opposite weeks
there's less drama and sometimes
that's lovely and relaxing but sometimes

we just miss those two, damn

Ode to the songs
we're singing
in our heads
in the silence
they're called earworms
and they're perfect renditions
every song
we could ever want to hear
playing on loop
somehow Johnny's got
Post Malone's exact vibrato
etched in his mind
season's change
and our love went cold
wait
how do our brains
do it so pitch-perfectly
run away
but we're running in circles
run away
run away
run away

[Educational field trips are permitted; see Christine in the front office for details.]

There's a gay club downtown, just a few blocks
from school. Denice is going to turn 18 soon,

so she could go on Thursday nights. The rest of us
will have to wait. Wouldn't it be great though,

all of us, together, at the club? None of us are 21,
obviously—even still, we will be high or drunk

with elation when we go, spider down the dark
streets, climb up light poles to get a better view

of this tragic town we're destined to flee. Denice,
Angel, and Johnny will show us the way

to dance-floor glory, while people in the shadows
of the bar emerge to spin us by the necks

like sparklers. We'll fly through the air, our bodies
trails of light spelling every identity we wish to claim.

Our head-back cackles will make the club-goers
think we haven't been fully impacted by suicide.

We'll save strobe-light flashes like Polaroids,
imprint our wild grins and sweaty chests.

Finn will stand on stage like a king, Vivian
will twirl incessantly in her purple flapper dress,

and Lexie will hold her arms out wide, embrace every
piece of night. And we will—we will—and we—

                              filter out of Room 404,

and into the vacant parking lot, a gray March day.
We grind our hands into the asphalt.

[Celebrate the successes of the group, no matter how small.]

Today's icebreaker
question: what's the one body
part you love the most?

We're back together
after spotty attendance.
Finally returned.

Angel pats his hair,
Denice flexes her biceps,
Finn points to their chin—

"Look!" We all lean in
close. It's a microscopic
chin hair. We all smile.

Lexie's feet flutter,
Vivian gives us spirit
fingers, purple nails.

Johnny stands and holds
his heart. He thump-thumps against
his chest. "Mine's right here."

Ms. Chase twirls her strand
of white hair and says: "Sometimes,
love takes convincing."

[The purpose of the group is to give support, not advice.]

Angel's having trouble

with the thought of telling

his mom he's gay.

"Mariconcito.

Inconceivable."

He says this

like it's the first time

he's heard either of those words.

We say, just do it. No,

that was Johnny. He's urgent,

pleading lungs. Angel's tight-

lipped. We're not happy

with the rogue nature of what's

happening today. We say,

she will understand,

give it time. No,

that was Vivian. We can't

all speak at once. His little

sister's name is Estrella—

Is that her?

Tap-dancing in the middle

of our circle? We put our phones

away, as much as we want

to go live. We look back

toward the guidelines we posted

months ago. Are those bats

hanging in the corner of the room?

Estrella's singing a charming ditty

about a toy trumpet

and a parade. We tell Angel

to keep that shit repressed

until he's 18. No,

that was Advice Guy™.

Ugh, seriously? He's here today?

We're putting our face in our hands,

looking down at the carpet. No,

that's Angel, hands twisting

up into his curly hair.

The bats are swarming

little Estrella now.

She tries to incorporate them

into her song and jig.

Will someone help us? Please?

Who? Is that Lexie?

Lexie, what's wrong?

We're having a panic attack—

we can't—get—air—

Please! Someone help us!

Is anyone going to help us?

Estrella is singing:

There they go, passing by!

Do we need to take her

to the hospital?

Can we drive? Does anyone

have a car? Who can?

Denice? We can. Johnny. OK.

Grab our hand. We're running out

into the hall. No,

that's Angel. Wow, he's fast.

Tell us what to do.

Deadass—someone tell us

what to do!

Just call her Dad!

Someone get his number!

We are out the door,

open door we didn't

close, open window we didn't

close, wind rushing

through the room,

empty, no one remembers

we were there and no one

knows we aren't there,

chairs in a circle, we are

one of the chairs

knocked over, location change

and didn't leave a note.

[Remember that some members may not feel
comfortable telling their parents about the group.]

We rush outside into the parking lot

where most of the cars have left for the day.

Denice wraps her arms around Lexie—

her gasps for air have slowed a bit now.

She's clutching her chest, hand beneath

an overall strap. When a green truck pulls up

and rolls the window down, we hear:

"Get in, Lexie. You're alright." Her dad

wears a Carhartt jacket and a John Deere hat.

He has deep lines around his eyes and a long beard.

"Are you all in band with her?"

Lexie's eyes grow big as cantaloupes,

her breaths accelerating again, and as Denice

helps her into the front seat, says,

"Oh yeah, I'm a drummer."

We're all in the parking lot, watching them

drive away, the words *thanks for taking care of her*

lingering in the air. It took us a while later

to realize Angel didn't stick around.

He sauntered off into the evening

in his puffy black jacket. He's heading home,

trying to decide whether or not tonight

is the night his life will change forever.

Should we go back to the meeting?

Where were we anyway?

[Supplemental meetings are permitted with administrative approval.]

    Every meeting we seem
    to end. We discuss love,
    which should never end,
    no? Love can't really die?
    It floats on. There was
    the plant Ms. Chase brought,
    already dead, told us
    it would liven up the room.
    She keeps watering it,
    every week, the water rushing
    out from the bottom.
    The year of each day swells
    when we're apart. We love
    each other, so we tread water.

[Make room for apologies when group members make mistakes.]

We're missing pieces today,
and we're here for the apology
from Lexie—she didn't mean to make
that last meeting all about her.

Ms. Chase says Lexie will have to apologize
again when Angel's here. Lexie acknowledges
that when Angel was being vulnerable,
she turned all the attention onto her
and broke the trust of the group.

***

In English class,
Angel was assigned an inquiry essay.
The topic he chose
was about symbols of freedom
in different cultures,
and his thesis centered on the arbitrary
and sometimes destructive
nature of these symbols.
Can a dirt bike be a symbol of freedom?
His paper argued yes, absolutely.

***

Endless doctors, psychologists, and tests run.
The taste of a popsicle stick
on a dry tongue.
Lexie feels everything so strongly.
She tells us that we're so connected.

"What you feel, I feel."
This apology is overflowing,
and we expected nothing less.

***

Family Feud plays on the living room TV,
and the couch feels scratchier than usual.
Angel's mom sits close
and pats his thigh.
"You are acting strange, hijo.
Do you want to talk about something?"

As Angel starts to speak, the sounds
of his little brothers fighting
break into the room, and his mom,
exasperated, goes to investigate.

Sometimes a breath invigorates,
sometimes a breath prepares

the body and mind
for action,
but mostly a breath
fills hollow lungs.

***

We continue on
because forgiveness is important,
Ms. Chase explains.

Lexie pledges to be better,
to not allow her tears—
"Straight, white tears," Denice interjects—
to take up space.

"We're not always
our best selves," Ms. Chase says.
"We are human, and we're just trying
to make our way through
this crazy world!"

We're only half-listening.

***

There's something
about after midnight,

about the wind whizzing past
the outline of a body,
the empty streets.
Sometimes your name
can sound foreign somehow,
although it's been your name
forever. Angel wears confidence
for a coat, wears memories
of taking his siblings
to the park down the street
as a helmet. He wonders
about the future—

is it really something

we create ourselves?

Or are we just

speeding down the road,

out of control,

completely missing

the newly installed speed bumps

all over town,

flying through the air

crashing into the unknown?

[Give advance notice if the meeting location
changes.]

Angel's hospital room is—fluorescent
and sterile. Ms. Chase brought yellow daisies

that burst against the white walls.
Angel lies under a light blue sheet,

and we stand in the entryway,
the faux-wood paneling beneath our feet.

"Oh my God! I can't believe
he's dying!" Lexie erupts into tears.

"I'm not dying, you idiot,"
Angel says groggily, waking up.

We come closer, stand around him
to form a circle with his hospital bed.

"I broke my leg, got some crazy bruises,
but your boy's a fighter."

He winks at Johnny.
Johnny blushes but stays tight-lipped.

"That's our guy," Denice says.
"I prayed so hard for you, Angel," Ms. Chase says.

We're all looking at Angel, smiling softly,
each of our breaths a relief for the lives

we have. There's a long silence, and then
Johnny pulls up a chair, sits down next to Angel

and takes his hand.

[Part 5]

[Reevaluate and reflect on the year thus far.]

We're forgetting the inception   again

          How often should we think

of the beginning   Should we put it

          on the calendar   Adam was just

one boy   and where do ghosts go   if they

          never had a home   to haunt

Seems logical   they would look

          for a place   to wander in circles

a makeshift home of their choosing   Should we let

          the ghosts come   embrace their desire

to be protected   despite the fact they'll never be

          enclosed again   like lungs

[Prioritize meetings even as the school year ends.]

Spring break ends and the school year
becomes a river. We're white-water rafting,
rushing past boulders, and, unlike
first semester, we call out commands,
and we're in control. Today, we don't hear

"Pass." Finn tells us he has a decision
to make: stay here with his aunt,
or go back to Virginia with his parents,
back to the trailer park,
back to the Appalachians.

We've been here before,
sat in the circle and nodded
our heads in unison, and we've seen
Finn, over and over again,
so his transformation comes

as a bit of a shock, the decisiveness,
and we are ready
to stop underestimating each other.
Despite our fragments, we are
whole, and Finn doesn't care

about the mountains

anyway. He wants to forget
the moment his parents
gave up on him. It's their loss.
He's here with us now.

[Admin Activity #5: Responding to common questions.]

Question #1: Who wears the pants in the relationship?	Question #2: How do you really know you're gay?
My style is none of your business, thanks.	The same way you know you're straight?
What do you mean? Both of us wear pants sometimes.	I'm not gay, I'm pan. Next question?
This question is misogynistic (spelling?), and I'm not answering.	I'm ACE. It means I'm not (usually) attracted to anyone. And that definitely includes you.
Anyone, regardless of gender identity, can be "powerful," if that's what you mean.	I'm trans, not gay. Sexual orientation and gender identity are different. You should
Wow, I've never heard that one before! Why don't you go back to Twitter, you homophobe.	do your own research before you ask ignorant questions.
	BOY BYE

Question #3: I know someone else gay! You two would be perfect for each other. Want me to set you up?	Question #4: Are you sure this isn't just a phase?
Wow, you know 2 gay people? I'm so happy for you. OMG! I know another straight person. You two would be perfect for each other. Want me to set you up? What makes you say that? What is it about the two of us that would make us perfect for each other? YES! But wait, are they rich?	Is your heterosexuality just a phase? Probably not, but so what if it is? Sexuality is fluid. That means that it changes over time. Sexuality isn't something I just try on for a day. It's a part of who I am. I hope not. I love being gay.

[Encourage participation in school-wide events.]

After affinity group, Johnny waits
for Angel in the mostly empty hallway.
There are still a couple of teachers around,
and the janitor cleans the glass
on the classroom doors.

"Hi," Johnny says.
His underarms are damp with sweat,
what a day to wear gray,
and he's got goosebumps.

"Sup," Angel says,
as he swings forward on his crutches.

"How are you feeling—your leg?"
Johnny gulps.

"Ah, I'm OK. I'm a little bummed.
I can't do track or anything now.
Maybe next year."

The janitor scoots between
Johnny & Angel
to clean the glass on the 404 door.

Johnny takes a heaping mouthful of air.
"Ok, so I have a lot of things to say.
First and foremost, I am so sorry
for pressuring you to tell your mom
about—you, and about—us.
That was wrong of me.
You should take all the time you need.
I'm so, so sorry.
Will you please forgive me?"

The janitor walks
back between them again, chuckling.
He nudges Angel lightly on the shoulder.
"He sounds sincere. I'd give him
another chance if I were you,"
he says, with a wink, before walking
off down the hallway.

The two boys let out a surprised laugh.

"It's cool, really," Angel says after a moment.
"I'm sorry, too.
I'm gonna tell her, eventually, but,
for now—let's take things slow, you know?"

"Totally! We can go
as slow as you'd like."

Angel faintly smiles, and Johnny
steps even closer.

"But you know, I'm kind of incapable
of going too slow, so I have to ask—
will you go to the spring dance with me?"

"Damn, that was short-lived," Angel laughs.

"I'm sorry!" Johnny exclaims, putting
his hands over his face.

"Nah, it's fine,
but I don't think we'd have very much fun
since I can't really dance right now."

"Oh my gosh, no, you're right.
I'm sorry, I shouldn't have asked."

Another teacher emerges from their classroom
with a student, discussing the make-up exam
they just took as they walk past.

"Although—"
a sly smile emerges on Angel's face,
and he swings back and forth on his crutches.
"I bet I could make it work,
you know, if you don't mind dancing

with a guy on crutches."

Johnny beams an enormous smile.
"I obviously don't mind!
Maybe we can invent some new dance moves?"

Angel winks.
"Can't wait."

Johnny moves close
and wraps his arms around Angel,
the hallway quiet,
their chests rising and falling
together in their embrace.

[Center mental health always, but especially as school gets stressful.]

This is the meeting where we can't even remember spring break because it feels like years ago, and summer feels nonexistent.

This is the meeting where we decide the teachers are conspiring against us. They decide to assign every exam and paper and project at the same time.

This is the meeting where Ms. Chase brings up the "Don't Say Gay" bills sweeping the nation. She explains it for those of us who've never heard. Could our group even exist if a bill like that passes?

This is the meeting where we wrangle with the fact that people say we can't teach little kids "these things" too young, and yet they plan a toddler boy and girl's wedding.

This is the meeting where we determine Mr. Martin is an asshole. He brought in a picture of his new baby boy, wearing a *lady killer* onesie, and he tells us that everything we do in life—our interests, our activities, the way we dress, the way we talk—is in order for us to procreate.

This is the meeting where Ms. Chase flips out. She's more outraged than we've ever seen her. She says she's going to tell Mr. Martin how problematic what he said really is.

This is the meeting where we start to like Ms. Chase. She feels like a leader today. She feels like an ally.

[Consider how you would describe the benefits of
the group to the rest of the school.]

Denice & Johnny head to the front of the auditorium.
Principal Jones has asked all the affinity groups
to share their experiences from the year.

We've heard from the White Allies Group,
the People of Color Affinity Group,
which included the Latinx, Black, and AAPI groups,

and we've heard from the Jewish Affinity Group,
and now—Wow, it's silent. There are so many
eyes, although lots looking down at phones.

We didn't really practice what to say.
We can tell them we started out as an ellipsis, omission,
things unsaid, pauses, a lack of utterance,

fear… and somehow what followed was
an interrobang, exclamation mark and question mark
jammed together, loud, excited, wondering.

We learned it's OK to be silent and OK to break
the silence with loud, clumsy questions and
dramatic emotions. We can say at first we wore

button downs, reserved, and now we're wrapping
neon feather boas extravagantly around our heads.
Maybe this will help them understand.

Maybe the reason we didn't practice
what to say is that there's really no way
of explaining us at all, and the only way

to fully understand our affinity
is to experience it firsthand.

[Advisors should feel free to organize social
gatherings outside of school.]

Everyone is rain,
and rain

touches nothing
tonight.

We hang
quietly in the air.

We are at Ms. Chase's house
for an end-of-the-year party.

Her place is nice,
with white string lights

wrapping the banister—
not like Room 404,

no cobwebs or the usual
circle with holes.

Remember when
we used to only call her

Middle-Aged
Straight White Lady?

We call her
Ms. Chase now, obviously.

She's grown on us.
We mean, she did

invite us to her home.
That was cool,

just a little awkward.
What are we doing here

again? In stagnant
air we hover,

fearful of breaking
across wood.

Where is the pizza?
Or the soda

or the cake?
Where is the tin roof

or the weather vane?

We hear Angel whisper,

"The fuck is this
vegan shit?"

The empty floors beg for
a simple patter,

then Lexie takes
a deep breath

and says to us:
"I don't know

anymore. I don't know
who I am, or who

I like." She looks
around the room.

"I just know I like
being around you all."

She's misty-eyed.
Vivian hugs her.

"It's OK
to not know.

It's OK
to not label things.

It's all OK."
Happy tears.

Ms. Chase grabs
the Kleenex.

Every week
we fraction ourselves

into parts small enough
to be understood.

Every week
we are recycled—

a problem
exists for decades,

discovers
a new body.

We form
small circles

in corners
of the house.

There's a sailboat
painting on the wall,

seagulls soaring
through blue sky.

What are they
looking for?

What are we
going to be

when the year
ends?

When will we
find answers

in the silence?
When will we

finally get to
eat some pizza?

[Make space to celebrate any graduating seniors.]

"Denice Claudia Brown."

Denice throws her fist into the air
after crossing the stage in her royal blue robe,

and her mom breaks down in tears. Even her dad
is there to hug her after she descends

the stage steps, an embrace each one of us
can feel from the back of the auditorium.

Most of us have never been to a graduation,
and we're all dressed up best as we can,

bow ties and church shoes, Vivian in a
purple dress, and Lexie in khakis and a yellow polo

decorated with daisies, the first time we've seen her
without her overalls. Outside the auditorium,

the sun is beating down on us, and Vivian's
stumbling in the grass, it's been a while

since she's worn heels, and Denice emerges
through the crowd with a beaming smile.

"Y'all made it! Thank you so much for coming!"
Denice's mom makes us get together for a group photo,

and we all put our arms around each other—
Denice, Vivian, Angel, Johnny, Finn, and Lexie.

Angel says, "What in the *hell* are we going to do
without you next year?" And Lexie chimes in:

"Yeah, there's no way we can do this without you!"
Denice wraps Angel in a massive bear hug,

crutches and all. We hear his back crack,
and then she turns to Lexie and does the same,

and Johnny joins in, then Vivian, and then
everyone yells at Finn to get his ass in here.

"Listen," Denice says pulling out of the group hug,
"I can't tell y'all how to get through next year,

or the year after that, or the year after that—
but I have a feeling you *all* will. Plus, I'm just

a phone call away." And now we're smiling and talking
and hugging in the bright sunshine, and we're

getting ready to be *not together*, and we hate
being nostalgic for the moment we're living

right now, but it's impossible, sometimes,
because being *together* in the group this year was

everything: monotonous yet glorious, sitting down
and bursting out of ourselves, listening to

the stories unique to our experiences. As Denice
is taking more pictures with her parents,

we remember the time she said *Y'all know*
I had no clue what was going on

leading the group the first few weeks—right?
But hey, we figured it out, together.

[Epilogue]

[Go around the circle one last time, for now.]

We are holding

hands, thanks to Ms. Chase,

and it feels

just a little weird,

but we don't hate it.

Late spring fills the room

with flowery air.

The spotted hawk's outside

our open fourth-floor window,

patient, calm, resting

on a thick, mossy branch.

Skin to skin, we are woven

together with letters:

an initialism

representing

each of us,

an aspect

of who we are,

of who we may become,

of something beautiful

we can claim.

It's the last Monday afternoon

of the school year,

and our eyes are fixed

on the blooming freedom

of summer.

This year, we contained

multitudes. We were

a polluted night sky,

purple and orange haze,

one or two stars.

We were a library—

people took books

and lost them

under their beds.

We were born

in an office, in a meeting

we weren't privy to.

We were living

on a fault line,

aftershocks
for days on end.

We were not

what people thought,

if people thought about us

at all.

We were a silent hallelujah

buried in the folds of our lungs.

We didn't choose

to exist—

we saw the sign on the door,

and we knocked.

[Acknowledgments]

Thank you to Erika Meitner for her encouragement of my "LGBT support group poems" from my days working on my MFA thesis at Virginia Tech. These were recurring poems that populated my thesis, and while they have taken on a completely different structure as a YA novel in verse, I am grateful for Erika's guidance and support of these poems—almost 10 years later they've manifested as this book.

Thank you to Lisa Summe for being the primary editor of this book and for always being a huge supporter of my writing. I sincerely appreciate all the poetic input she has given me over the years.

Thank you to *Lammergeier* and *Watershed Review* for publishing select poems from this novel, both in different forms. Thank you to Jamie Beth Cohen, Emanuel Xavier, and Lisa Summe for writing such kind blurbs about the book. Thank you to Alyssa Mason for helping to craft and edit the book description.

Thank you to Kat Flores for illustrating the cover and the section divide sketches. Since working together on Syracuse University's LGBT publication *The OutCrowd*, I have been a huge fan, and I am grateful for their exceptional artistic eye and creating visuals that perfectly encapsulate the spirit of the book.

Thank you to Sven Davisson of Rebel Satori Press for continuing to believe in my work and for giving this book a home.

Thank you to all my friends, family, and my partner for being strong supporters of my work and allowing me the time and grace to pursue my passion of writing.

[Notes]

The epigraph of this book comes from Alex Dimitrov's poem "Love" from his book *Love & Other Poems*.

The poem "[First, begin with the group guidelines.]" directly quotes language from PFLAG's support group guidelines resource posted on their website in 2015.

The poem "[Stay on task and be an active listener, even if it's difficult to do so.]" references the novel *The House on Mango Street* by Sandra Cisneros.

The poem "[Don't be afraid to speak up; vulnerability is key.]" is dedicated to Mariana Sierra.

The poem "[Encourage round-robin participation for any group activities.]" is dedicated to Matteo Iudice.

The poem "[Being an active listener means re-focusing when your mind wanders.]" is after Mark Bibbins and uses language from his poem "7-Minute Song" from his collection *Sky Lounge*.

The poem "[During extended breaks, make sure members have a way to connect.]" is dedicated to the Tidbits Snap Café.

The worksheet "[Admin Activity #4: Flipping the Coin.]" is borrowed from Catherine Griffith's work titled "It Gets Better: A Group Experience for LGBTQ Youth."

The worksheet "[Admin Activity #4: Flipping the Coin.]" uses lyrics from Cardi B's song "Bodak Yellow."

The poem "[If any members become chronically absent, check in on them.]" uses lyrics from Post Malone's song "Circles."

The poem "[The purpose of the group is to give support, not advice.]" uses lyrics from Shirley Temple's song "The Toy Trumpet."

The poem "[Encourage participation in school-wide events]" is dedicated to Lisa Summe.

In the first and last poems in the book, there is a spotted

hawk, and I hope it is the same hawk as the one in Walt Whitman's "Song of Myself," verse 52: "The spotted hawk swoops by and accuses me, he complains of my gab and my loitering. // I too am not a bit tamed, I too am untranslatable, / I sound my barbaric yawp over the roofs of the world."

www.ingramcontent.com/pod-product-compliance
Lightning Source LLC
Chambersburg PA
CBHW022042090426
42741CB00007B/1163